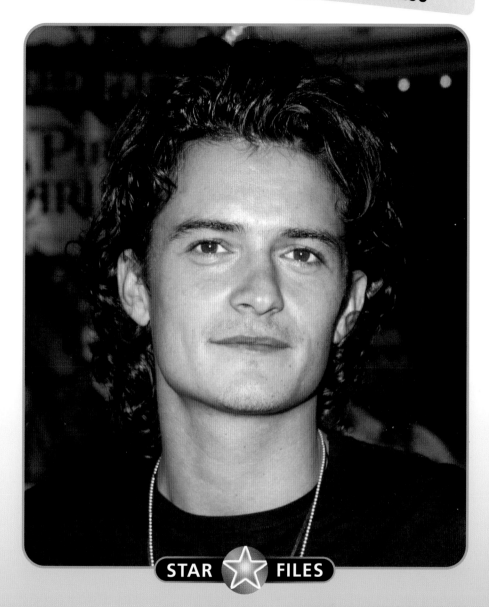

STAR FILES

Orlando Bloom

Kay Barnham

www.raintreepublishers.co.uk
Visit our website to find out more information about **Raintree** books.

To order:
☎ Phone 44 (0) 1865 888113
🖹 Send a fax to 44 (0) 1865 314091
🖥 Visit the Raintree Bookshop at **www.raintreepublishers.co.uk** to browse our catalogue and order online.

Produced for Raintree by
White-Thomson Publishing Ltd
Bridgewater Business Centre
210 High Street, Lewes, BN7 2NH

First published in Great Britain by Raintree,
Halley Court, Jordan Hill, Oxford OX2 8EJ,
part of Harcourt Education.
Raintree is a registered trademark
of Harcourt Education Ltd.

Editorial: Nicola Hodgson,
Sarah Shannon, and Kate Buckingham
Design: Tinstar Design Ltd (www.tinstar.co.uk)
and Michelle Lisseter
Picture Research: Nicola Hodgson
Production: Chloe Bloom

Originated by Modern Age
Printed and bound in China by
South China Printing Company

10 digit ISBN 1 844 43284 X
13 digit ISBN 978 1 844 43284 4
09 08 07 06
10 9 8 7 6 5 4 3 2

**British Library Cataloguing in
Publication Data**
Barnham, Kay.
Orlando Bloom. – (Star Files)
791.4′ 3′ 028′ 092

A full catalogue record for this book
is available from the British Library.

Acknowledgements
The publishers would like to thank the following
for permission to reproduce photographs: Allstar
Picture Library pp. **9** (b), **10** (l), **11**, **12**, **14**, **15**,
16 (l), **16** (r), **17**, **18**, (l), **18** (r), **27**, **29**, **39** (b),
40; Corbis pp. **4**, **8**, **10** (r) (Jim Ruymen/Reuters),
22 (b), **33** (b), **39** (t); Getty Images pp. **6**, **30** (t),
31 (t), **31** (b), **33** (t) (Stephen Shugerman/Stringer),
35 (l) (Jim Ross/Stringer), **35** (r); Retna Pictures Ltd
pp. **7** (l) (Grayson Alexander), **7** (r) (Adrian Boot),
13 (r) (Sara De Boer), **25** (r) (Gregorio Binuya),
26 (l) (Gina James/Graylock.com), **32** (Grayson
Alexander), **37** (Tammie Arroyo), **38** (r) (MLC),
41 (t) (John Spellman), **43** (Ernie Stewart); Rex
Features pp. **5** (Stephen d'Antal), **9** (t) (Erik C
Pendzich), **13** (l) (New Line/Everett), **19** (Simon
Runting), **20** (Everett Collection), **21**
(Focus/Everett), **22** (t) (AXV), **23**
(Universal/Everett), **24** (Walt Disney/Everett),
25 (l) (Walt Disney/Everett), **26** (r) (Warner
Br/Everett), **28** (New Line/Everett), **30** (b) (Eric
Ford), **34** (New Line/Everett), **36** (Chris
Hatcher/BEI), **38** (l) (Charles Sykes), **41** (b) (Eric
Ford), **42** (Miramax/Everett). Cover photograph
reproduced with permission of Corbis.

Quote sources: p. **5** www.etherealattic.co.uk;
pp. **7**, **11**, **43** *Orlando Bloom: the Biography* by
A. C. Parfitt; pp. **8**, **12**, **16**, **21**, **32**, **36**
www.theorlandobloomfiles.com; p. **10**
Ed Wilson, Artistic Director, National
Youth Theatre; p. **23** www.visimag.com;
p. **29** www.perfectpeople.net; p. **31**
www.allmovieportal.com; p. **35** interview
with Orlando Bloom on *So Graham Norton*,
1 March 2002, Channel 4, United Kingdom;
p. **39** www.ctv.ca; p. **40** www.timesonline.co.uk

The publishers would like to thank Sarah
Williams, Charly Rimsa, Catherine Clarke,
and Caroline Hamilton for their assistance
in the preparation of this book.

Every effort has been made to contact the
copyright holders of any material reproduced
in this book. Any omissions will be rectified
in subsequent printings if notice is given to
the publishers.

The paper used to print this book comes
from sustainable resources.

Disclaimer: This book is not authorized
or approved by Orlando Bloom.

Contents

Any words appearing in the text in bold, **like this**, are explained in the glossary. You can also look out for them in the "Star words" box at the bottom of each page.

Elf, boxer, pirate, outlaw

Orlando Bloom is one of the most popular actors in the world. When his name appears on a film poster, it means that the film is likely to be a success. When Orlando goes to a film's **premiere**, there are crowds of fans waiting for him. During his short **career**, Orlando has played some very different **roles**.

ALL ABOUT ORLANDO

Full name: Orlando Bloom (also known as Orli or OB)
Born: 13 January 1977
Place of birth: Canterbury, Kent, England
Family: Harry (stepfather), Sonia (mother), Samantha (older sister), Colin Stone (birth father)
Height: 5 feet 11 inches (1.8 metres)
Marital status: single
Big break: appearing in the film *Wilde* in 1997
First major film: *The Lord of the Rings: Fellowship of the Ring* (2001)
Other interests: photography, sculpting, extreme sports such as skydiving and snowboarding

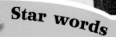

In *The Lord of the Rings*, he was an elf. In *Pirates of the Caribbean*, he was a pirate. He has also acted as a boxer, an **outlaw**, and a prince. Which parts will he play next? One thing is for sure – Orlando is always ready for the next challenge.

"I've been an elf ... a boxer, a pirate and an outlaw. I really am living every boy's dream."

Who did Orlando play in *The Lord of the Rings*?

Orlando has lots of fans around the world!

What part did Orlando play in *Troy*?

In which film does Orlando appear with Kirsten Dunst?

premiere first showing of a film, often with celebrities invited
role part that an actor plays in a film, play, or television show

Young Orlando

Canterbury Cathedral is a beautiful building.

Orlando Bloom was born in Canterbury. This is a small, historic city in the south-east of England. He lived there with his parents and his sister. Orlando did not have a showbusiness upbringing. He had a happy, normal childhood.

Famous father

Orlando's father was Harry Bloom. Harry was born and grew up in South Africa. He believed that the way South Africa was run was wrong, and he spoke out against it. Black and white people were made to live apart. Black people were very poor and had very few rights. When Harry wrote novels about how wrong he felt this to be, he was thrown in prison. In 1963, he and his wife moved to England. Sadly, Harry Bloom died in 1981, when Orlando was just 4 years old.

A film star's name

Orlando Bloom's real name is... Orlando Bloom! He is named after a 17th-century **composer** called Orlando Gibbons. Orlando's parents chose a name that everyone would remember. That is a good thing for a film star!

Star fact

Orlando is not the only actor in the family. Orlando's older sister, Samantha, went to the Guildhall School of Music and Drama in London. Will Samantha be as famous as her brother in the future?

Star words   composer person who writes music

Orlando had two fathers – Harry Bloom and Colin Stone.

Family friend
Harry Bloom worked with the famous African leader, Nelson Mandela (see below). They were in prison together, too. Mandela was in prison for 27 years. He was finally released in 1990. He always fought for the rights of black people in South Africa. He was the country's first black president, from 1994 to 1999.

Boy with two fathers

When Orlando was 13 years old, his mother gave him some surprising news. She told Orlando that Harry Bloom was not his real father. Orlando's father was Colin Stone. Colin had been a family friend for many years. When Harry Bloom died, Colin had become Orlando's **guardian**. Orlando was shocked by his mother's news. He kept the fact about his real father a secret for many years. Now, Orlando is pleased that he had two fathers.

> I don't know any family that doesn't have a little story somewhere.

guardian someone who is not your real parent but who is responsible for looking after you

A creative student

When he was young, Orlando was not very interested in school. He did not want to be in a classroom. He preferred to be outside. Also, he had mild **dyslexia**. This meant he found it quite hard to read. Then Orlando found subjects that interested him. He enjoyed studying art, sculpture, and photography. He loved drama, too.

> Don't laugh at your mates when they have problems with reading. Maybe they'll become movie stars and you'll want tickets to their premieres!

On the stage

Orlando's first taste of fame as a teenager was reading poetry at a local festival. This was good practice. Orlando soon found that speaking in front of a crowd was not scary. At school, he got the chance to act. His drama teacher says that

On television

Orlando's favourite television programmes were *The A-Team* and *Knight Rider*. In these programmes, the heroes fought against evil. Orlando wanted to be just like them.

Orlando enjoyed studying photography.

Star words   dyslexia condition where someone finds it difficult to read

Orlando would play any **role.** He was just happy to be on stage. Orlando took part in his school's performance of *The Pirates of Penzance*. This was a musical play by the famous 19th-century British **composers** called Gilbert and Sullivan.

To be a hero

Orlando loved tales of action and adventure. The *Superman* films were his favourites. Orlando wanted to be a hero like Superman. Then he found out that Superman was not a real person, but an actor. Orlando was surprised, but he was not disappointed. If he could not be a hero, he would be an actor. Then he could play the part of a hero!

Christopher Reeve starred as Superman.

Superman
Christopher Reeve (see above) was a famous actor. He starred in four *Superman* films from 1978 to 1987. Christopher Reeve was **paralyzed** in a riding accident in 1995. He worked hard on behalf of disabled people. Sadly, he died in 2004. To many people, he was a hero on screen and a hero in real life.

paralyzed when someone cannot move a part of their body

A star in waiting

Orlando was determined to become an actor. When he was sixteen, he was given the chance to follow his dream. He won a **scholarship** for the National Youth Theatre in London. Orlando left Canterbury to head off to the capital city.

Following the stars

Many famous actors went to the National Youth Theatre. Academy Award winner Daniel Day-Lewis studied there. You can see him in the picture above as the star of the film *The Last of the Mohicans*. Timothy Dalton studied at the National Youth Theatre too. He is famous for playing the part of James Bond.

Not just acting

The National Youth Theatre teaches students all about the theatre. They learn much more than just acting. There are lessons in lighting, sound, scenery, and costumes. Orlando loved his lessons. One of his teachers later said, "Orlando was one of the finest young performers we've ever had."

> ★ **Star fact**
>
> When he moved to London, Orlando's favourite hobby was going out to nightclubs.

Hollywood star Kevin Spacey has taught at the British American Drama Academy, where Orlando studied.

Star words

scholarship when a student is given money to help them go to a school or college

Another scholarship

Orlando acted in lots of plays at the National Youth Theatre. A **talent scout** spotted him in one performance. It was Orlando's lucky day. He was offered another scholarship, to the British American Drama Academy. This is a very highly respected college in London. At the academy, students from around the world learn about acting on stage. They are taught by leading actors such as Sir Ben Kingsley, Kevin Spacey, and Jeremy Irons.

A TV role

Orlando got an agent. It is an agent's job to find work for an actor. Orlando soon won parts in television programmes. He appeared in the popular UK hospital drama *Casualty*. Orlando played the part of a patient. He also had small parts in the drama series *Midsomer Murders* and in the comedy show *Smack the Pony.*

Orlando's favourite actors:

- Daniel Day-Lewis
- Johnny Depp
- Paul Newman
- Ed Norton

Orlando says of Johnny Depp, "Johnny's been a ... guideline for me as a young actor..."

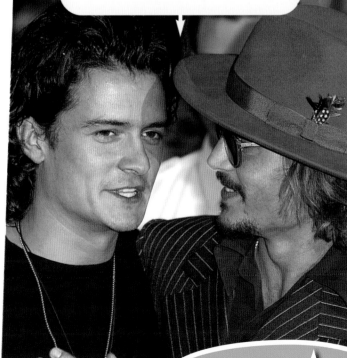

talent scout someone who looks out for talented performers such as actors, models, or athletes

11

Ewan McGregor

The talented Scottish actor Ewan McGregor went to the Guildhall, like Orlando. He has starred in lots of successful films, including *Star Wars: Episode 1 - The Phantom Menace.*

A big break

Orlando continued his training at the Guildhall School of Music and Drama when he was eighteen. The school teaches musicians, actors, and people who want to work in the theatre. Orlando spent three enjoyable years there and earned his university degree.

> I was 22, I had 2 more days of drama school and it was like, 'Here! Have a **career**!' Boom!

While at the Guildhall, Orlando had his first big break. He was offered a part in *Wilde*. This was a film about the famous 19th-century poet and **playwright** Oscar Wilde. *Wilde* starred well-known British actors Stephen Fry and Jude Law. Orlando only had a small part in the film, but people noticed him.

Back to school

After Orlando appeared in *Wilde*, he had many more offers of work in films and television programmes. Orlando was not ready for this. He decided that it was more important to finish his training. He gained more experience by acting in lots of plays.

Ewan McGregor played the young Obi-Wan Kenobi in *Star Wars.*

Star words

audition interview for an actor or musician, where they show their skills

An even bigger break

Near the end of his time at the Guildhall, Orlando **auditioned** for Peter Jackson. He was a film **director** from New Zealand. Then, 2 days before Orlando **graduated** from the Guildhall, something amazing happened. Orlando was offered the **role** that was to change his life. It was the part of Legolas. This was one of the main characters in *The Lord of the Rings*.

Peter Jackson (left) chose Orlando to star in *The Lord of the Rings*.

Jude Law

One of the stars of *Wilde* was Jude Law (see above). This famous English actor has been in more than 30 films. He has acted with Gwyneth Paltrow, Nicole Kidman, and Renée Zellweger. Perhaps he and Orlando will act together again one day...?

director person in charge of making a film
graduate pass exams and leave a school or college

The elf prince

★ ★ ★ ★ ★ ★ ★ ★

Tolkien's tales

The Lord of the Rings is a novel written by J. R. R. Tolkien (1892–1973). It was published in the 1950s. The Lord of the Rings is often said to be the most popular novel in the world. It has been translated into many languages.

★ ★ ★ ★ ★ ★ ★ ★

The role of Legolas won Orlando a place in cinema history. *The Lord of the Rings* films were some of the most successful ever made. The three films were **nominated** for 30 Academy Awards. They won an amazing seventeen awards.

Adventures in Middle-earth

The Lord of the Rings is an **epic** story that is loved by readers of all ages. It is set in an **imaginary** land called Middle-earth. The main character of the story is Frodo, a hobbit. Hobbits are small creatures who look a bit like humans with furry feet. Frodo's uncle gives him a magic ring. This ring must be destroyed before it falls into the hands of the evil Lord Sauron. If Sauron gets the ring, Middle-earth will be ruined. Frodo must take the ring to Mount Doom and throw it into the fiery volcano there. That is the only way to break Sauron's power.

The Fellowship of the Ring was the first film of the **trilogy.**

Star words

epic long story, poem, or film
imaginary make believe

Peter Jackson (left) chats to actress Liv Tyler, who played Arwen.

The Fellowship of the Ring

Luckily, Frodo has eight friends to help him in his adventure. There is Gandalf the wizard. Sam, Pippin, and Merry are three hobbits. Aragorn and Boromir are humans. Gimli is a dwarf. Finally, there is the elf, Prince Legolas. This is the character that Orlando Bloom brings to life on screen. The nine characters are known as the Fellowship of the Ring.

 Star fact

The three *The Lord of the Rings* films took almost US$3 billion (£1.54 billion) at box offices around the world.

The director

Peter Jackson had always loved *The Lord of the Rings*. He was delighted when he got the chance to direct the films. Peter was given an Academy Award for Best Director in 2004. He won the award for the third film – *The Return of the King*.

nominated put forward as one of the right people (or, sometimes, films) to win an award

Samurai warriors

Orlando prepared well for *The Lord of the Rings*. He watched films about **samurai** warriors. Orlando tried to act in a calm and focused way, just like them. *The Seven Samurai* (1954) is one of his favourite films (below).

An action hero

Orlando had to spend 2 months training for *The Lord of the Rings*. Legolas the elf is a very sporty character. He is an expert at **archery**. He can ride a horse without a saddle. He is very good at sword fighting, too. Orlando had to practise all of these skills before filming started.

Star fact

Orlando became very good at firing arrows. He could hit paper plates that his trainers threw into the air.

Copycat

Orlando also had to learn how to move smoothly and gracefully. He watched how cats walked, ran, and jumped. Then he tried to copy them. Next time you watch the films, watch Legolas closely. As he leaps and springs out of danger, does he remind you of a cat?

> Elves are ... graceful and elegant like cats... That's how I tried to be.

Star words

archery shooting using a bow and arrow. Archery is just a sport now, but it used to be an important way of fighting

A new language

In *The Lord of the Rings*, the elves speak a language called Elvish. The language was invented by the author – J. R. R. Tolkien. Orlando and other members of the cast learned how to speak Elvish words.

Becoming an elf

Legolas Greenleaf looks very different from Orlando Bloom. This meant that Orlando had to spend hours getting ready every day. Make-up artists totally changed the way he looked. They hid his brown curly hair beneath a long blond wig. Blue contact lenses covered his brown eyes. Orlando also wore extra-pointy elf ears!

Working with stars

Many well-known actors starred in *The Lord of the Rings* **trilogy**. Sir Ian McKellen has appeared in many films and plays. In *The Lord of the Rings*, he plays the part of Gandalf the wizard.

Orlando learned a lot from watching Sir Ian McKellen act.

samurai warrior or soldier in ancient Japan, well known for being brave and noble

17

Filming in New Zealand

The Lord of the Rings films were made in New Zealand. This beautiful country has many different types of landscapes. There are snow-topped mountains, rainforests, and **fiords**. The **director** of the films, Peter Jackson, is from New Zealand. He thought his country was just like Middle-earth.

The film brought lots of business to New Zealand. Many local people worked as **extras** on the film. *The Lord of the Rings* increased New Zealand's tourism. People now visit New Zealand to see where the filming took place.

Aragorn

Viggo Mortensen (above) played Aragorn. He and Orlando became great friends off set as well as on screen. They went fishing and surfing together. Their nicknames for each other were "elf boy" and "filthy human".

New Zealand was the perfect place to film *The Lord of the Rings*.

Star words

extra person who appears in crowd scenes in a film. Extras are not usually given lines to speak.

The actors in *The Lord of the Rings* became close friends while they were filming.

A fellowship of actors

The Lord of the Rings films were all made at the same time. It took 18 months to shoot all 3 films. The cast and crew lived in New Zealand while filming took place.

New Zealand is more than 18,000 kilometres (11,180 miles) away from the UK. This meant that Orlando was a long way from his home and family during filming. However, he enjoyed his time in New Zealand. Orlando became friends with his fellow actors. They had a lot of fun together.

Fellowship

Cast members were tattooed with a special symbol. This was the number nine in Tolkien's language of Elvish. They chose this symbol because there were nine members of the Fellowship of the Ring. The tattoo would remind the actors of their time in New Zealand and of their friendship.

fiord narrow and rocky inlet of the sea

Lord of the box office

★ ★ ★ ★ ★ ★ ★ ★

Black Hawk Down

In 2001, Orlando appeared in *Black Hawk Down*. This was a realistic war film. It starred popular actors Josh Hartnett, Eric Bana, and Ewan McGregor. Orlando played the part of a young soldier. The film was very popular in the United States.

When *The Lord of the Rings* came out, audiences loved it. **Directors** loved it, too. They wanted to cast Orlando in their own films. Now, Orlando could pick which film **roles** to play.

A careful choice

Orlando Bloom had played the same character in three films. Now, he needed to show audiences that he was not just an elf in a blond wig. Orlando needed to show that he was a **versatile** actor. Orlando soon made a decision. He agreed to play an Australian **outlaw**. The film was called *Ned Kelly*. It came out in 2003.

Orlando played the part of a young soldier in *Black Hawk Down*.

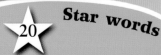

Star words

versatile a versatile actor is one who can play many different kinds of characters

Success Down Under

Ned Kelly is based on a true story. In the film, Orlando played the part of Joe Byrne. He was a member of the Kelly Gang. These Australian outlaws took part in daring bank robberies. They lived during the 19th century. The part of Ned Kelly was played by the popular Australian actor Heath Ledger.

> " It was so rewarding playing a character who was a hero in real life to so many Australians. "

The film was not a big hit. However, it was very popular in Australia, where it made more than AUS$5 million. This was 86 per cent of the total box office takings in Australia in 2003.

Following their daring exploits, the Kelly Gang became Australian folk heros.

21

A leading role

Orlando's next film was called *The Calcium Kid*. This was a totally new type of film for him. A big Hollywood studio did not pay for the film. It cost £160 million to make *The Lord of the Rings* **trilogy**. *The Calcium Kid* had a **budget** of less than £0.51 million.

Orlando stars as Jimmy Connelly. He is a milkman who boxes in his spare time. Then Jimmy accidentally injures the local boxing champion. Jimmy is persuaded to take his place. The only problem is that Jimmy has to fight the world champion… His friends believe he can win. They think that the calcium in the milk he drinks will make him super-strong!

★ Star fact

In real life, Orlando prefers soya milk to cow's milk. Soya milk is made from soya beans.

Guest stars

Frank Bruno and Chris Eubank (above) were once world-champion boxers. Both men appeared in *The Calcium Kid*. They did not play parts, though. They played themselves.

In *The Calcium Kid*, Orlando's character loves to drink milk!

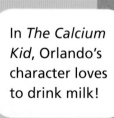

Star words   budget amount of money it costs to do something

Home sweet home

For Orlando, one of the best things about *The Calcium Kid* was the location. The film was made in South London. This meant that Orlando could live at home during filming. He enjoyed living near his friends.

A small success

The Calcium Kid was not a huge hit. However, it was very popular with Orlando's fans. He enjoyed playing a funny **role**. Orlando's comedy skills would come in useful in one of his next films.

66 I'm very proud of this film, because it offered an opportunity for me to be a bit of a clown. 99

Orlando plays a boxer in *The Calcium Kid.*

Comedy time

The Calcium Kid did not have a lot of famous stars. For the first time, Orlando played the leading **role**. Better still, he got the chance to act in a comedy.

Johnny Depp is a very well-known actor.

Pirates ahoy!

Orlando's next part was a **swashbuckling** one. He starred in *Pirates of the Caribbean: The Curse of the Black Pearl*. In this film, Orlando plays a **blacksmith** called Will Turner. He finds out that his father was a famous pirate, and his life changes forever.

In this film, Orlando is a hero once again. His character discovers that it might be more fun being a pirate than a blacksmith. He fights with a sword. He swings from ships' **rigging**. He takes part in daring adventures. He also has plenty of comedy moments. In the film, it looks as if all the actors are having a fantastic time!

Captain Jack Sparrow

Johnny Depp is a very experienced actor. He has starred in more than 40 films. In *Pirates of the Caribbean: The Curse of the Black Pearl*, he plays the part of Captain Jack Sparrow. He was **nominated** for an Academy Award for the **role** in 2004.

Filming in the Caribbean

Much of *Pirates of the Caribbean* was filmed in the Caribbean. Outdoor scenes were shot on the Caribbean island of St Vincent. The indoor scenes were filmed at Disney's studios in California.

⭐ Star fact

Pirates of the Caribbean was inspired by a Disney theme-park ride.

Star words   blacksmith person who makes iron tools by hand

More adventures

The film was an enormous success. Its makers decided to make not one, but two **sequels.** The stars of the film, Johnny Depp, Orlando Bloom, and Keira Knightley, all agreed to take part.

Making films can be very expensive. Like *The Lord of the Rings* **trilogy**, the two films were made at the same time. This saved money.

Orlando Bloom and Keira Knightley watch as Jack Sparrow escapes.

Elizabeth Swann

Keira Knightley (below) is a popular young British star – just like Orlando. In *Pirates of the Caribbean*, she plays the part of Elizabeth Swann. Will Turner and Elizabeth Swann fall in love. Will they end up together...?

rigging ropes that support a ship's mast and sails
swashbuckling daring and adventurous

25

The Trojan War

Orlando's next **role** was in the **epic** *Troy*. This came out in 2004. The film was based on a long poem by the ancient Greek poet Homer. The film is about the **legendary** war between the Greeks and the people of Troy.

Eric Bana and Orlando played brothers in *Troy*.

Helen of Troy

In *Troy*, Diane Kruger (above) plays the part of the beautiful Helen. Diane was not always an actress. First, she was a ballet dancer. After an injury, she became a fashion model. She made her first film in 2002. In 2004, she starred with Josh Hartnett in *Wicker Park*.

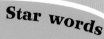

complex very complicated

Orlando starred as Paris, a prince of Troy. Paris falls in love with a beautiful woman called Helen. She runs away with him. Unfortunately, Helen is already married to a Greek king. Her husband wants her back. So the Trojan War begins...

A challenging role

In other films, Orlando had played brave heroes. He was used to fighting and winning. The part of Paris was much more **complex**. Now, Orlando had to play a character who was both loved and hated. Paris could be blinded by love. He could be foolish. He could also be a coward. Orlando rose to the challenge. This was the type of meaty role he had been waiting for.

Trojan Horse

Troy has a cast of fantastic actors. However, one cast member is very wooden indeed. It is a very large wooden horse! The Trojan Horse is used to smuggle Greek warriors into Troy.

Location, location, location

The story of *Troy* is set in ancient Greece. However, *Troy* was actually filmed on the island of Malta. The film brought lots of money to the Mediterranean island. Extra scenes were shot in Mexico.

Fellow pin-ups

Orlando Bloom was not the only good-looking actor in *Troy*. He had lots of competition! Brad Pitt (above) played Achilles – a handsome warrior. Eric Bana played Paris' brave brother, Prince Hector. Eric starred in the film *Hulk*. He and Orlando had already acted together, in *Black Hawk Down*.

legendary described in stories from long ago

Danger man!

Horsing around

When filming *The Lord of the Rings*, it was very important that Orlando did not hurt himself. Any injuries would delay filming. This would cost extra money. Unfortunately, Orlando's horse fell on to him. Orlando cracked a rib. Luckily, he was soon back in the saddle.

Orlando Bloom likes to take risks. He loves to do hair-raising stunts and extreme sports. Unfortunately, his activities have often landed him in trouble. He has broken his back, his ribs, his nose, both of his legs, his arm, his wrist, a finger, and a toe. He has also cracked his skull three times.

A rooftop accident

Orlando's worst accident happened in 1998. He was just 21. He tried to open a rusty door on to a roof terrace. To do this, he climbed up an outside wall. A drainpipe pulled away from the wall and Orlando fell. He broke his back. Doctors spent hours operating on him. They fitted two plates to his **spine**. The doctors were worried that Orlando might never walk again. However, he walked out of the hospital on crutches just 12 days later.

Orlando is a good rider, but this has not prevented him from having accidents!

Star words

safety harness set of straps and ropes that stop someone from falling

Getting better

It took Orlando a long time to recover from the accident. He had to wear a back brace for a year. The accident also changed him emotionally. Orlando now thinks he is more mature and more determined to succeed. His aches and pains from the accident remind him how lucky he is to be alive. However, he still enjoys extreme sports!

> I'm rather accident-prone, I have to admit.

Stuntman

Orlando performed many of his own stunts in *Pirates of the Caribbean* (above). He swung through the **rigging**. He was high above the ship's deck. However, this was not too dangerous. Orlando wore a **safety harness** to make sure he did not fall.

spine series of bones that reach from the skull to the bottom of the back

Orlando will jump on to a board wherever there is surf.

Extreme sports

Orlando loves surfing. He also enjoys white-water rafting, snowboarding, and skydiving. Orlando took part in all of these activities when he was filming in New Zealand.

He told *The Lord of the Rings* cast members that he enjoyed extreme sports. Elijah Wood (Frodo) and Viggo Mortensen (Aragorn) thought that he was joking. These sports sounded far too dangerous. It was not long before Orlando had persuaded Elijah and Viggo to come surfing with him! Soon, they learned to love the sport, too.

Surf dude

Orlando learnt to surf in New Zealand. Back home, he surfs in Cornwall, in the south-west of England. He says that the water is much colder there! Orlando still surfs with his friends from *The Lord of the Rings* whenever he can.

Not all of Orlando's sports are extreme!

Star words bungee jumping sport of leaping from a high place with a stretchy rope tied around the ankles

Orlando likes to go snowboarding.

Bungee jumping

The sport of bungee jumping is thousands of years old. People of the Pacific Islands still dive from wooden towers. They do not tie bungee ropes to their legs. Instead, they use vines. Boys jump to show that they have become men.

Aaaaarrrghh! Bungee jumping

New Zealand is one of the most exciting places in the world to **bungee jump**. There are many famous jumps. People jump from bridges and into canyons.

As soon as Orlando got to New Zealand, he went bungee jumping. He did not jump straight away. He stood on the platform for an hour. Then he took a deep breath – and dived. Now bungee jumping is one of his favourite sports.

> " I love to ... do kind of crazy stuff which is slightly outrageous... "

Bungee jumping is now popular around the world.

31

Behind the scenes

Kate's films

Kate Bosworth made her first film, *The Horse Whisperer*, when she was fifteen. In 2002, she starred in the surf movie *Blue Crush*. In 2004, she starred with Hollywood star Kevin Spacey in *Beyond the Sea*. She also starred in *Win A Date with Tad*

Orlando likes to talk about his films, but he keeps his personal life private. You will not find Orlando chatting about his love life on the pages of a celebrity magazine! He says, "I try to keep my private life separate from my **professional** life."

Orlando's girlfriends?

Orlando will not answer questions about his girlfriends, past or present. However, he and actress Kate Bosworth dated for a few years. Kate is 6 years younger than Orlando. She was born on 2 January 1983. Kate is from Los Angeles in the United States – the home of Hollywood. There were **rumours** that the couple would marry. However, they split up in 2005. They were both so busy working that they did not spend much time together.

Kate Bosworth is a popular film star, just like Orlando.

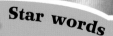

Star words

professional something to do with a person's job

Favourite foods

Pasta

Pizza

Porridge

Rice

Spinach

Baked potatoes

Orlando went to the US **premiere** of *Beyond The Sea* with Kate.

From clubbing to chilling out

When he was younger, Orlando loved to go out with his friends. He often went to nightclubs. Now, he does not have much time off. When he is not working, he prefers to relax. Orlando likes to walk along beaches. Sometimes, he likes to do nothing at all!

On the move

Orlando has been in demand ever since he left drama college. He has rushed from one film set to another. When Orlando filmed *The Lord of the Rings*, he spent 18 months in New Zealand. He has also filmed in the United States, Australia, Malta, Mexico, and the Caribbean.

One of Orlando's favourite foods is pizza.

rumour story that lots of people discuss, but that may not be true

A man's best friend

Orlando loves dogs. He once owned a dog called Maude. Then Orlando had to spend a lot of time filming in New Zealand for *The Lord of the Rings*. He was never at home to look after his dog. Orlando gave Maude to someone who did not have to travel so much. In 2004, he and Kate Bosworth adopted two stray dogs, called Siti and Guero.

A blond disguise

The Lord of the Rings made Orlando Bloom famous. Afterwards, he found that he could still walk down the street without fans spotting him. So why was this happening? It was all because of Legolas the elf. Many people thought that Orlando really had long blond hair and blue eyes. They did not recognize the actor with the dark, curly hair and brown eyes!

Fan-tastic!

Orlando now has millions of fans around the world. Every week, he receives sacks of fan mail. He does not have time to reply to all of the letters. Through his fan club, he thanks everyone who has written to him.

After he starred as Legolas, Orlando's fans thought that he had blond hair, too!

34

Star words

technophobe someone who is scared of technology, such as computers and email

Orlando was the top attraction at the 2004 Toronto International Film Festival.

Orlando does not like to let his fans down. Crowds of Orlando's fans went to the Toronto International Film Festival in September 2004. The star signed so many autographs that the showing of his new film, *Haven*, was delayed.

Internet-free zone

Orlando Bloom does not like computers. He does not own a computer. He does not have an email address. However, Orlando's mum does like computers. She lets her famous son know of any interesting information that she finds on the Internet. Sonia Bloom at last managed to persuade Orlando to have his own official website. It went live in 2005.

I'm a technophobe...

Football fan

Orlando is a fan of Manchester United, the football team. He is also a fan of top football player David Beckham (above). Orlando supports whichever team David plays for. David now plays for the Spanish team called Real Madrid.

A true Tolkien fan

Orlando had never read *The Lord of the Rings* before he played the part of Legolas the elf. He has now read the book many times. Even after shooting three films, this is still one of his favourite books!

A cool dresser

When he was training to be an actor, Orlando needed to earn money. He used to work in **second-hand** clothes shops. He bought his own clothes there, too. Although he could not afford much, Orlando began to develop his own style. Now he enjoys buying the clothes he likes, however much they cost.

"There was a time I could only look at the stuff in the shops, but now I can buy the outfits I really like."

Addicted to jewellery

As well as cool clothes, Orlando loves to wear jewellery. He is often spotted wearing rings, necklaces, and watches. Look closely at photos of Orlando. He is often wearing unusual pieces of jewellery.

Orlando is a big fan of weird and wonderful jewellery.

Star words   second-hand something that was once owned by someone else

Favourite films

The Hustler (1961)
with Paul Newman

Stand by Me (1986)
with River Phoenix

Amélie (2001) with
Audrey Tautou

Orlando has a wacky sense of style. His clothes are never boring.

When Orlando was filming in New Zealand, a make-up artist gave him a special ring. It is a copy of the famous ring from *The Lord of the Rings* films.

A sparkly present

Orlando also likes to give jewellery as presents. There are **rumours** that Orlando gave Kate Bosworth a diamond ring worth US$340,000 (£175,000).

What's next?

Orlando Bloom is now one of the most popular film stars in the world. His film **roles** are becoming more and more challenging.

A darker role

The part Orlando plays in *Haven*, which was released in 2004, is very dark. His character lives on the Cayman Islands in the Caribbean. He becomes involved with two criminals. Then he commits a crime that affects a whole country.

Haven gave Orlando a new view of film-making. As well as playing one of the main parts, he was also one of the **producers** of the film. Like *The Calcium Kid*, *Haven* was made by a small independent company.

Top bachelor

People Magazine is a US celebrity magazine. Every year, the magazine lists Hollywood's hottest **bachelors**. In 2004, the winner was Orlando Bloom. He beat both Ashton Kutcher and Prince William to the top spot.

Orlando at the **premiere** of *Haven* with co-star Bill Paxton (left) and the film's **director**, Frank E. Flowers.

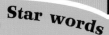

Star words   bachelor man who is not married

Haven was filmed in the Cayman Islands in the Caribbean.

Famous co-star

Liam Neeson stars with Orlando in *Kingdom of Heaven*. Liam is a very experienced actor. He has starred in many fantastic films. These include *Star Wars: Episode 1 - The Phantom Menace* (see below), *Schindler's List, Rob Roy,* and *Love Actually.*

Cool outfit

Orlando really enjoyed filming *Haven*. He did not have to spend hours getting ready for his role. There were no heavy costumes. There were no wigs. Orlando did not even have to learn how to sword fight. Instead, his outfit was a pair of shorts.

> It was really hot there so wearing shorts ... was great.

From *Haven* to *Heaven*

Orlando was taken back in time once again for his next film. *Kingdom of Heaven* is set in the 12th century. Orlando plays the part of a **blacksmith**. He protects his people against foreign invaders. The cast includes Eva Green, Liam Neeson, and Jeremy Irons. One of Orlando's all-time acting heroes, Ed Norton, also appears in the film.

producer film producers organize the people and money to make a film

A life in cinema

Kirsten Dunst started acting when she was three. She has appeared in more than 40 films. At the age of twelve, she starred with Tom Cruise in *Interview with the Vampire.* Kirsten is best known for the *Spiderman* films. She plays Mary Jane Watson, Spiderman's girlfriend.

Romance blooms

Orlando's next film was *Elizabethtown.* This came out in 2005. Kirsten Dunst stars as Orlando's love interest. Susan Sarandon plays his mother.

Elizabethtown is a comedy-drama, with a touch of romance. Orlando plays the part of a shoe designer called Drew Baylor. Drew makes a mistake that costs his company millions of dollars. Then he is fired. Then his girlfriend dumps him. Sadly, his father dies at the same time. Drew returns home for the funeral. He also goes to carry out his father's dying wishes. While flying home, Orlando meets an air hostess. Suddenly, Drew's life takes a turn for the better.

> I'd love to be playing dark character roles ... but it's about what scripts you get.

Kirsten played Mary Jane Watson, Spiderman's girlfriend.

Bond, James Bond?

In 2005, a new James Bond novel was published. This was written by Charlie Higson. He is a popular UK comedian. The book is about James Bond's early life. There are **rumours** that there will be a film version of the book. There are also rumours Orlando Bloom will star as the young James Bond. Hollywood insiders say that Orlando will play the famous character before he became a secret agent. This would be a treat for Orlando's fans!

Orlando enjoyed filming *Elizabethtown*. Will he enjoy playing James Bond one day?

Hollywood star

In her long **career**, Susan Sarandon (above) has acted in more than 70 films. She has been **nominated** for four Academy Awards. In 1995, she won the Best Actress award for *Dead Man Walking*. Susan keeps this award in her bathroom!

Hamlet

Hamlet tells the story of Prince Hamlet. His father has died and is now a ghost. The ghost tells Hamlet that his father was murdered. Hamlet does not know what to do. Is the ghost telling the truth? Should Hamlet kill the murderer?

To be or not to be?

When he was training to be an actor, Orlando appeared in many plays. Since **graduating**, he has spent his time in front of film cameras. He has not appeared in any more plays. However, he has said that he would love to play the part of Hamlet.

Hamlet was written by William Shakespeare. This **complex** and **tragic** tale is a very popular play. The **role** of Prince Hamlet is difficult and challenging. Perhaps this is the right part to persuade Orlando Bloom to go back to the stage?

Many famous actors have played Prince Hamlet, including Mel Gibson in a 1990 film.

Star words   cinemagoer person who goes to the cinema

★ ★ ★ ★ ★ ★ ★ ★ ★

Farewell to Legolas

After *The Return of the King*, Orlando took off his elf ears for the last time. This was a very sad moment for him. Orlando had spent 18 months being Legolas. If he had the chance, it is one part that Orlando would love to play again.

★ ★ ★ ★ ★ ★ ★ ★ ★

21st-century star

So what does the future hold for Orlando Bloom? He has played many roles already. Hopefully he will play a great many more. He may return to the stage. He may continue to delight **cinemagoers**. There might even be an Academy Award waiting for him! Only time will tell.

> ❝ Do I want to be a pin-up? Do I want to be just a poster boy? No, I don't. ❞

tragic very sad

Find out more

Books

Lovin' Bloom, Heather Kranenburg
(Ballantine Books, 2004)
Orlando Bloom: The Biography, A. C. Parfitt
(John Blake, 2004)

Filmography

Pirates of the Caribbean 3 (2007)
*Pirates of the Caribbean: Dead Man's
Chest* (2006)
Elizabethtown (2005)
Kingdom of Heaven (2005)
Haven (2004)
Troy (2004)
The Calcium Kid (2004)
*The Lord of the Rings:
The Return of the King* (2003)
Ned Kelly (2003)
*Pirates of the Caribbean:
The Curse of the Black Pearl* (2003)
*The Lord of the Rings:
The Two Towers* (2002)
Black Hawk Down (2001)
*The Lord of the Rings:
The Fellowship of the Ring* (2001)
Wilde (1997)

Awards

Here are just some of the many awards Orlando Bloom has won so far:

2004 MTV Movie Awards: Sexiest Hero

2004 Screen Actors Guild Awards: Outstanding Performance by a Cast for *The Lord of the Rings: The Return of the King*

2003 Hollywood Film Festival Awards: Hollywood Breakthrough Award – Male Performer

2003 GQ Men of the Year Awards: Best Film Actor

2003 AOL Moviegoer Awards: Best Supporting Actor for *The Lord of the Rings: The Two Towers*

2002 MTV Movie Awards: Best Breakthrough Performance for *The Lord of the Rings: The Fellowship of the Ring*

2002 Empire Awards Best Debut for *The Lord of the Rings: The Fellowship of the Ring*

Websites

To find out more about Orlando Bloom and his films, try these websites:

http://www.theofficialorlandobloomsite.com
Orlando's official website packed with the latest information.

http://www.theorlandobloomfiles.com
A website full of interviews, articles and video clips featuring Orlando.

Disclaimer

All the Internet addresses (URLs) given in this book were valid at the time of going to press. However, due to the dynamic nature of the Internet, some addresses may have changed, or sites may have ceased to exist since publication. While the author and publishers regret any inconvenience this may cause readers, no responsibility for any such changes can be accepted by either the author or the publishers.

Glossary

archery shooting using a bow and arrow. Archery is just a sport now, but it used to be an important way of fighting.

audition interview for an actor or musician, where they show their skills

bachelor man who is not married

blacksmith person who makes iron tools by hand

budget amount of money it costs to do something

bungee jumping sport of leaping from a high place with a stretchy rope tied around the ankles

career what someone does for a job

cinemagoer person who goes to the cinema

complex very complicated

composer person who writes music

director person in charge of making a film

dyslexia condition where someone finds it difficult to read

epic long story, poem, or film

extra person who appears in crowd scenes in a film. Extras are not usually given lines to speak.

fiord narrow and rocky inlet of the sea

graduate pass exams and leave a school or college

guardian someone who is not your real parent but who is responsible for looking after you

imaginary make believe

legendary described in stories from long ago

nominated put forward as one of the right people (or, sometimes, films) to win an award

outlaw old-fashioned word for someone who breaks the law or who is a criminal

paralyzed when someone can not move a part of their body

playwright someone who writes plays

premiere first showing of a film, often with celebrities invited

producer film producers organize the people and money to make a film

professional something to do with a person's job

rigging ropes that support a ship's mast and sails

role part that an actor plays in a film, play, or television show

rumour story that lots of people discuss, but that may not be true

safety harness set of straps and ropes that stop someone from falling

samurai warrior or soldier in ancient Japan, well known for being brave and noble

scholarship when a student is given money to help them go to a school or college

second-hand something that was once owned by someone else

sequel film or book that continues an earlier story

spine series of bones that reach from the skull to the bottom of the back

swashbuckling daring and adventurous

talent scout someone who looks out for talented performers such as actors, models, or athletes

technophobe someone who is scared of technology, such as computers and email

tragic very sad

trilogy series of three related books, plays, or films

versatile a versatile actor is one who can play many different kinds of characters

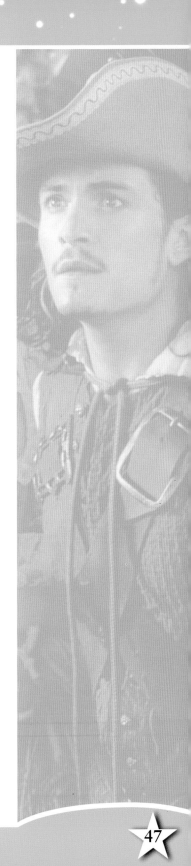

Index

Titles in the *Star File* series include:

Johnny Depp
Jane Bingham
Hardback   1 844 43283 1

Beyoncé Knowles
Mark Stewart
Hardback   1 844 43296 3

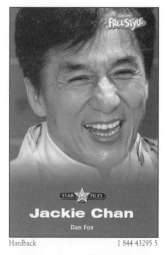

Jackie Chan
Dan Fox
Hardback   1 844 43295 5

Usher
Dan Whitcombe
Hardback   1 844 43298 X

David Beckham
Paul Harrison
Hardback   1 844 43297 1

Andre Benjamin
Brian Fitzgerald
Hardback   1 844 43972 0

**Mary-Kate and
Ashley Olsen**
Stephanie Fitzgerald
Hardback   1 410 91662 6

Orlando Bloom
Kay Barnham
Hardback   1 844 43284 X

Find out about other titles in this series on our website www.raintreepublishers.co.uk